Freemasonry

and

Christianity

Alva J. McClain, Th.M., D.D., LL.D.

Founder and First President,
Grace Theological Seminary

BMH Books
Winona Lake, Indiana 46590

First Printing, 1951
Second Printing, 1955
Third Printing, 1959
Fourth Printing, 1963
Fifth Printing, 1968
Sixth Printing, 1977

Cover Design: Paul Woodruff

ISBN: 0-88469-041-5

COPYRIGHT 1969
BMH BOOKS
WINONA LAKE, INDIANA

Printed in U.S.A.

FOREWORD

This sermon was prepared while Dr. Alva J. McClain was pastor of the First Brethren Church of Philadelphia, Pennsylvania. Several young men of that church were being urged by friends to enter the Masonic lodge, and they came to Dr. McClain for counsel in the matter. As the outcome of a conference with them, he promised to make a fair investigation of the organization on the basis of such Masonic literature as might be accessible to the general public, and to report his findings in the form of a sermon to the church congregation. Following the delivery of the sermon to a large audience, a number of interested friends made provision for its publication requesting that it be printed as delivered with as little change as possible. This will explain the conversational manner.

This booklet has had wide circulation, having gone through five printings. In order to bring the documentation up-to-date, the references to the *Encyclopedia of Freemasonry* were taken from the "New and Revised Edition" published by the Masonic History Company in 1924.

BMH Books sends forth this, the sixth printing, with the prayer that this important message by the late Dr. Alva J. McClain might serve in an increasing ministry of helpfulness to persons being confronted by Freemasonry, and as Dr. McClain himself said in an earlier foreword, "that its ministry may be used to

3

open the eyes of men, that they may see and honor
the Lord Jesus Christ as 'the true God, and eternal
life' (I John 5:20)."

BMH Books
1977

FREEMASONRY AND CHRISTIANITY

By Alva J. McClain

I have two texts: Matthew 12:30—"He that is not with me is against me"; John 12:48—"He that rejecteth me, and receiveth not my words, hath one that judgeth him: the word that I have spoken, the same shall judge him in the last day."

Will you listen carefully while I present three propositions?

(1) *Jesus Christ is God manifest in the flesh, and apart from Him the true God can neither be known, worshiped, nor acknowledged.*

(2) *Salvation is by faith in the atoning blood of the Lord Jesus Christ, apart from all human works and character.*

(3) *It is the supreme obligation of every saved person to obey the Lord Jesus Christ in all things.*

These three propositions are the pillars of the Christian faith—the deity of Christ, salvation by faith in Him, obedience to His Word. Do you believe these three things? I am going to ask every person who does to stand! [Nearly the entire congregation stood.] Thank you! I knew you believed them, but I can preach to you better after that testimony.

About four weeks ago I called over the telephone one of the highest officers of the Grand Lodge, at

5

his office at the Masonic Temple in Philadelphia. I told him frankly that I was not a Mason and that I desired to obtain some authentic information regarding Freemasonry and its religious position. This officer suggested three books by Masonic authorities. I told him that one would be sufficient, and asked him which of the three books was the best. Without hesitation he answered, "Get the *Encyclopedia of Freemasonry,* by Mackey. It is, without question, our highest and best authority." He then referred me to a man at the Masonic Library. I called him and asked him for the highest and most authentic Masonic authority. Without a moment's hesitation he answered, "Get the *Encyclopedia of Freemasonry,* by Mackey." I have that encyclopedia with me here tonight. In the main, my analysis of Freemasonry will be based upon its statements and claims. Surely, no Mason can question the fairness of this method.

The author of this encyclopedia, Albert G. Mackey, is one of Masonry's most learned and famous men. Besides being a Thirty-Second Degree Mason, he held many high offices in the organization. At the writing of this work he was "Past General Grand High Priest of the General Grand Chapter of the United States." Practically his whole life was devoted to research work on behalf of Masonry. His industry was amazing! A stream of books came from his pen, among which are *A Lexicon of Freemasonry, Manual of the Lodge, The Book of the Chapter, A Text Book of Masonic Jurisprudence, Cryptic Masonry, The Symbolism of Masonry,* and *The Masonic Ritualist.* This encyclopedia, however, is the crowning work of his life. He was engaged in its preparation for 30 years.

This encyclopedia contains about a thousand pages, with articles upon almost every conceivable subject that is in any way related to Freemasonry. During the past four weeks I have gone through the book carefully and have read hundreds of its articles. I am impressed with the exhaustive manner with which the author treats the various subjects. Certainly I am not in agreement with the doctrines of the institution which Dr. Mackey defends, but that does not keep me from admiring his able scholarship, his painstaking research work, his sober and fair presentation of Masonic subjects. And my admiration increases when I remember the extreme difficulty under which Dr. Mackey was compelled to prepare his encyclopedia. The authors and editors of other encyclopedias never faced such a difficulty. Dr. Mackey was expected to give to the public the fullest possible exposition of Masonry and at the same time reveal none of its *secret work.* In spite of this difficulty, Mackey has produced a monumental work and all Masons may justly point to the man with pride.

My examination of Freemasonry tonight will be absolutely from the viewpoint of a Christian. I have nothing to say to Masons who are not Christians. If I were not a Christian, I would undoubtedly be a Mason tonight, as I was preparing to enter when the Lord Jesus saved my soul. I am speaking to those who own Jesus Christ as Lord and God.

I shall not assume to speak for Freemasonry tonight—*Freemasonry shall speak for itself*. By its own utterances, by its own words, Freemasonry must stand justified or condemned. Matthew 12:37 —"For by thy words thou shalt be justified, and by thy words thou shalt be condemned."

I. Masonry Claims To Be a Religious Institution.

This claim is made not once in this encyclopedia, but literally dozens of times in different articles. We have not the time to hear all these references. I shall ask you to hear only one. Under the article on "Religion," Dr. Mackey discusses fully the right of Masonry to be called a "religious institution." He says that some of the more "timid brethren" have been afraid to declare its religious character lest the opponents of Masonry should use this fact against the lodge. But he insists that the truth should be told. I quote from the encyclopedia (pp. 618-619):

I contend, without any sort of hesitation, that Masonry is, in every sense of the word except one, and that its least philosophical, an eminently religious institution—that it is indebted solely to the religious element which it contains for its origin and for its continued existence, and that without this religious element it would scarcely be worthy of cultivation by the wise and good. But, that I may be truly understood, it will be well first to agree upon the true definition of religion. There is nothing more illogical than to reason upon undefined terms.

Dr. Mackey then gives in full Webster's definition of "religion." The quotation is too lengthy to give in full, but Dr. Mackey proves conclusively that Freemasonry meets every requirement of Webster's three primary definitions of religion, and sums up the proof in the following words:

Look at its ancient landmarks, its sublime ceremonies, its profound symbols and allegories—all inculcating religious doctrine, commanding religious observ-

ance, and teaching religious truth, and
who can deny that it is eminently a religious institution? . . .

Masonry, then, is indeed a religious institution; and on this ground mainly, if
not alone, should the religious Mason
defend it.

This should settle for all time the question as
to whether or not Freemasonry is religious. According to its own claims, it is proper to speak of
the "religion of Freemasonry." The man who con-
tends that Freemasonry is not a "religious institution" is childishly ignorant of the organization or
else he is a willful deceiver! Masonry is religious
—it teaches religion. But this fact does not neces-
sarily condemn Freemasonry.

Now I desire to lay down a Biblical truth—
an axiom of Christianity. Here it is: *There is only
ONE true religion. That religion is Christianity.
All other religions are false.*

I need not argue that proposition. No Christian
has ever denied it. But listen to the word of the
Lord Jesus himself on this point. Jesus said, "I
am the door." The door to what? The door to God;
the door to heaven; the door to eternal life. But that
is not all. Listen to this same Jesus as He con-
tinues: "All that ever came before me are thieves
and robbers" (John 10:7-8).

We are now in a position where we can determine absolutely whether or not the religion of Freemasonry is false or true. Here are the propositions:

There is but one true religion—Christianity!

Freemasonry has a religion!

If it is Christianity, it is true!

If it is not Christianity, it is false!

The issue is perfectly clear. The logic of these propositions cannot be evaded. We shall now go to Masonry's highest authority and say: "You have told us that your institution is a religious institution. We believe you, but we would ask you one more question. Is your religion Christianity or is it not Christianity?" Freemasonry has answered this question. Mark carefully the answer on page 618 of the encyclopedia:

> The religion of Freemasonry . . . is not Christianity!

These are not *my* words! They are the words of Masonry's own encyclopedia, prepared by one of the greatest Masonic authors, recommended to me as authentic by one of the highest officers of the Grand Lodge in Philadelphia! It declares Freemasonry has a religion, and that religion is not Christianity!

I have not condemned Freemasonry. Freemasonry has condemned itself!

11

Let us use a little logic here: If the religion of Freemasonry is not Christianity, then it is false! If the religion of Freemasonry is false, then it is not of God! If the religion of Freemasonry is not of God, then it is of the evil one!

Does any man care to stand up and say that a Christian can belong to and support an institution which teaches a religion which is not Christianity? If so, let him face the apostle Paul, who said: "But though we, or an angel from heaven, preach any other gospel unto you than that which we have preached unto you, let him be accursed. As we said before, so say I now again, If any man preach any other gospel unto you than that ye have received, let him be accursed" (Gal. 1:8-9). The curse of God is upon every religion outside of Christianity.

I might pronounce the benediction and go home, but there is more to be said.

II. Freemasonry Rates Christianity as a "Sectarian Religion" While Boasting of Its Own "Universality."

Again I quote from the encyclopedia:

The religion of Masonry is not sectarian. It admits men of every creed within its hospitable bosom, rejecting none and

12

approving none for his peculiar faith. It is not Judaism . . . it is not Christianity . . . (p. 619).

It does not meddle with sectarian creeds or doctrines, but teaches fundamental truth (p. 618).

If Masonry were simply a Christian institution, the Jew and the Moslem, the Brahman and the Buddhist, could not conscientiously partake of its illumination; but its universality is its boast. In its language, citizens of every nation may converse; at its altar men of all religions may kneel; to its creed, disciples of every faith may subscribe (p. 439).

I came here tonight determined to discuss this subject of Masonry deliberately and calmly, but I find it difficult in the face of the audacious blasphemy of such statements and claims as I have read! Can you, as a Christian, sit unmoved by such a dastardly comparison between Christianity and Masonry? According to this noted Masonic authority, Christianity is a sectarian religion! Christianity can be compared with Mohammedanism, Buddhism, and Brahmanism! Masonry cannot be compared with these religions! Christianity teaches a sectarian creed! Masonry teaches a creed of fundamental religious truth!

13

Do I need to tell this audience that all these great swelling words are a lie? If you want the truth, just reverse all these statements! It is the religion of Masonry that is sectarian! Christianity is the universal religion! It is the religion of Masonry that belongs down in the market place alongside of Buddhism, Brahmanism, and Mohammedanism! Christianity belongs above them all!

Oh, you Christians here tonight, is our Christ only a sectarian Christ, deserving only of a place alongside of these false prophets? Is that blessed faith which He came to inaugurate by His sinless life, His atoning death, His resurrection from the dead—is this faith, after all, only a sectarian faith like that of Mohammed and Buddha? I tell you, *No!* But let the Bible answer.

"I saw in the night visions, and, behold, one like the Son of man came with the clouds of heaven, and came to the Ancient of days, and they brought him near before him. And there was given him dominion, and glory, and a kingdom, that all people, nations, and languages, should serve him: his dominion is an everlasting dominion, which shall not pass away, and his kingdom that which shall not be destroyed" (Dan. 7:13-14).

"Behold the Lamb of God, which taketh away the sin of the world" (John 1:29).

"And I, if I be lifted up from the earth, will

draw all men unto me" (John 12:32).

"He is the propitiation for our sins: and not for our's only, but also for the sins of the whole world" (I John 2:2).

"Wherefore God also hath highly exalted him, and given him a name which is above every name: that at the name of Jesus every knee should bow . . . And that every tongue should confess that Jesus Christ is Lord, to the glory of God the Father" (Phil. 2:9-11).

III. Masonry Does Not Confess Jesus Christ as Lord and God. Therefore, the God of Masonry Is Not the True God.

Masonry has a god—you can't have a religion without a god. And this god has a name. Over and over in this encyclopedia you meet with the initials "G.A.O.T.U." This is the god of Masonry. The initials stand for the name "Great Architect of the Universe." This is the god that the Masons worship at their altar. This is the god to whom Masonic prayers are offered. Sometimes other names are applied to him, but, according to Mackey, "G.A.O.T.U." is the technical Masonic name for him (pp. 290, 310).

Now I shall present the Christian view of God. Every intelligent Christian is acquainted with it, but let us refresh our minds. I shall present it in three statements:

(1) *There is only one true God.* This one true God exists in three Persons—Father, Son, and Holy Spirit. But there are not three Gods. There is only one God, indivisible in substance and being.

(2) *This one true God became incarnate in the flesh and is none other than Jesus Christ.*

"In the beginning was the Word, and the Word was with God, and the Word was God. . . . And the Word was made flesh, and dwelt among us, (and we beheld his glory, the glory as of the only begotten of the Father,) full of grace and truth" (John 1:1, 14).

"Philip saith unto him, Lord, shew us the Father, and it sufficeth us. Jesus saith unto him, Have I been so long time with you, and yet hast thou not known me, Philip? he that hath seen me hath seen the Father . . ." (John 14:8-9).

"We know that the Son of God is come, and hath given us an understanding, that we may know him that is true, and we are in him that is true, even in his Son Jesus Christ. This is the true God, and eternal life" (I John 5:20).

(3) *The one true God cannot be confessed, honored, acknowledged, worshiped, believed on, or prayed to, apart from Jesus Christ!*

"Whosoever denieth the Son, the same hath not

the Father . . ." (I John 2:23).

"That all men should honour the Son, even as they honour the Father. He that honoureth not the Son honoureth not the Father which hath sent him" (John 5:23).

This is the Christian doctrine of God. Let me sum it up briefly: There is one true God. This true God is revealed in the Person of Jesus Christ. Apart from Christ there is no true God. If a man confesses Jesus Christ, he is confessing the true God. If he worships Jesus Christ, he is worshiping the true God. If a man refuses to confess Jesus Christ as God, he is denying the true God. If he refuses to worship Jesus Christ, he is refusing to worship the true God.

Now we are ready for the question, "Is the god of Masonry the true God, or is he a false god?"

The answer depends absolutely upon Masonry's attitude toward Jesus Christ! If Masonry asks its initiates to acknowledge and confess Jesus Christ as Lord and the true God, then Masonry's god is the true God. But if Masonry does not require its members to confess and acknowledge Jesus Christ as Lord and the true God, then the god of Masonry is *not* the true God! There is no escape from one of these two conclusions. Which conclusion is right should be apparent to the merest novice.

Masonry has thousands of members who would

never have entered it if they had to confess Jesus Christ as Lord and God to get in—the Jewish members, for instance. But let Masonry speak for itself (p. 619):

THERE IS NOTHING IN IT [MASONRY] TO OFFEND A JEW! (emphasis mine).

Do you know what this means—"There is nothing in Masonry to offend the Jew"? Let me tell you—Jesus Christ one day came to the Jews and said, "I and my Father are one." The Jews promptly picked up stones to stone Him. "Jesus answered them, Many good works have I shewed you from my Father; for which of those works do ye stone me? The Jews answered him, saying, For a good work we stone thee not; but for blasphemy; and because that thou, being a man, makest thyself God" (John 10:30-33).

The Jews condemned Jesus Christ to death and delivered Him to the Romans for crucifixion because He claimed to be their own God, the mighty Jehovah! To this day the Jews regard Christianity as a blasphemous religion because we worship and confess Jesus Christ as Lord and God.

I tell you, if there is nothing in Masonry to offend the Jew, then Masonry does not confess Jesus Christ as Lord and God, nor ask its initiates to do so. And if Masonry does not confess Jesus

18

Christ, then Masonry does not confess the true God. And if Masonry does not confess the true God, then Masonry confesses a false god. And if Masonry confesses a false god, let us be plain and call Masonry what it really is, by its own utterances, in the light of the Bible—nothing but *paganism and idolatry!*

This is the exact teaching of the Bible. All worship and acknowledgment paid to any god apart from Jesus Christ is idolatry. "And we know that the Son of God is come, and hath given us an understanding, that we may know him that is true, and we are in him that is true, even in his Son Jesus Christ. This is the true God, and eternal life. Little children, keep yourselves from idols" (I John 5:20-21). "Be not deceived: neither fornicators, nor idolaters . . . shall inherit the kingdom of God" (I Cor. 6:9-10).

But someone may say: "It is true that Jesus Christ is not confessed in the first three degrees, but He is confessed as God in some of the higher degrees of Masonry."

Well, I will have to take your word for it. This Masonic encyclopedia contains articles on almost every false god of the pagan world, but it contains not even the trace of an article on Jesus Christ, the Son of God. This is a significant and ominous omission.

But suppose it is true that Christ is recognized as God in some of the higher degrees, such as the Knights Templar. What of it? Does that clear the skirts of the organization? Let me ask you a question: Can you reach those higher degrees, can you become a Knight Templar without passing through the first three degrees? No, you cannot! That settles the question. Will any intelligent, enlightened Christian affirm that it is permissible to become an idolater first in order that afterward he may be a Christian? Will he affirm that it is right first to bow the knee at the altar of a false god in order that afterward he may bow the knee to the true God? Will Jesus Christ accept a confession of His deity from the mouth of a man whose lips are defiled with the confession of a false god? How foolish!

Suppose a Buddhist should come to me and say: "We have an organization we would like you to join. In order to take the first three degrees, you will have to acknowledge a god, but not your Christ. Afterward we will fix up a place in the organization and invent some new degrees where you Christians can get together and confess your Christ."

Suppose I should start an organization here in this church with secret work and several degrees. The first three degrees would eliminate the name of

Jesus Christ and demand that every candidate confess a god named "G.A.O.T.U." We would accept Christians, Jews, Mohammedans, Buddhists. After they had passed the first three degrees, we would say: "Now, if you Christians want to get together and confess your Christ, go up in a room by yourselves. You Mohammedans do the same, and so forth. But don't drag your peculiar views into these three degrees."

That's what Masonry does. What a pitiful sop to throw to our blessed Lord Jesus Christ! As a Christian, I spurn it.

But all this discussion is altogether unnecessary. The encyclopedia declares that—

> The germ and nucleus of all Free-
> masonry is to be found in the three primi-
> tive degrees (p. 753).

And only last week a Thirty-Second Degree Mason, a friend of mine, said to me: "When a man has taken the first three degrees, he is as much of a Mason as he can ever be! All the higher degrees are merely additions, superfluous."

Oh, the insult of it! To exclude Jesus Christ from the main building of Masonry, the foundation and basis of Masonry, and then to offer Him a place in a side room along with Mohammed, Buddha, and the rest of the "thieves and robbers." Masonry had better left Him out altogether than to offer

21

Him this crowning insult. Even if some of His professed followers seem to be strangely blind, Masonry ought to have known that Jesus Christ would accept no place at all unless it be the place of *preeminence*. Colossians 1:18 declares that "in all things" Christ must have "the preeminence." Masonry refuses Him the place of preeminence; therefore Masonry is a Christless institution!

Masonry even goes so far as to mutilate the Word of God in order to exclude Jesus Christ. I have here another work by the author of the encyclopedia. It is called "The Masonic Ritualist." Don't get excited—it is not "The Ritual." It doesn't contain any of the secrets. According to the author, it contains "all that may be lawfully taught in print of the degrees." It gives the prayers and Scriptures which are to be read in the opening and closing of the lodge. Every Scripture used is emptied of Jesus Christ, but there is a particularly glaring mutilation on page 271. I shall give the quotation exactly as it appears in the "Ritualist" followed by the author's explanatory note:

CHARGE TO BE READ
AT OPENING THE LODGE

Wherefore, brethren, lay aside all malice, and guile, and hypocrisies, and envies, and all evil speakings.

If so be ye have tasted that the Lord is gracious, to whom coming as unto a living stone, disallowed indeed of men, but chosen of God, and precious; ye also as living stones, be ye built up a spiritual house, an holy priesthood, to offer up sacrifices acceptable to God. . . .

(The passages of Scripture here selected are peculiarly appropriate to this degree. . . . The passages are taken, with slight but necessary modifications, from the second chapter of the First Epistle of Peter. . . .)

You will note that Dr. Mackey says some "slight but necessary modifications" have been made in these Scriptures. What are these "modifications"? Let me read I Peter 2:5 from the Bible and you will see.

"Ye also, as lively stones, are built up a spiritual house, an holy priesthood, to offer up spiritual sacrifices, acceptable to God *by Jesus Christ*" (italics mine).

Do you see it? The name of Christ is struck out by the profane hand of Masonry! And mark you, this is said to be a "slight modification"! And still further, it is said to be a "necessary modification"! Certainly it is necessary, because Masonry pretends to be able to approach God and offer

23

service to Him without coming through Jesus Christ! There are in this "Masonic Ritualist" 28 prayers, and not one of them is offered in the name of Jesus Christ!

This is the insolent answer of Masonry to the ultimatum of Christ—"No man cometh unto the Father, but by me" (John 14:6).

Now I am ready to classify Freemasonry in the light of its own utterances and statements of the Word of God.

Masonry admits that it confesses a god, but does not confess Jesus Christ. Let me read you one passage—I John 4:3 ASV—"Every spirit that confesseth not Jesus is not of God: and this is the spirit of the anti-christ, whereof ye have heard that it cometh; and now it is in the world already." These are not my words. These are the words of God. Do you dare, as a Christian, wear the emblem of such an organization?

IV. Before Accepting Any Christian as a Member, Masonry Demands That He Disobey Jesus Christ.

Obedience to the Lord Jesus Christ is the first and supreme duty of every Christian. Christ said in John 14:15, "If ye love me, keep my commandments." And I John 2:3 and 4 declares: "And hereby we do know that we know him, if we keep his commandments. He that saith, I know him, and keepeth not his commandments, is a liar, and the truth is not in him."

Now let me read you something that was commanded by the Lord Jesus in the most solemn manner. "Swear not at all; neither by heaven; for it is God's throne: nor by the earth; for it is his footstool: neither by Jerusalem; for it is the city of the great King" (Matt. 5:34-35). Our Lord considered this thing so tremendously important that He caused it to be written a second time in the Scripture (James 5:12). Nothing is more plain in the Bible. The Christian is commanded by the Lord to swear not at all by any oath. The government of the United States recognizes this and makes provision for Christians who believe in following the precept of the Lord. No Christian is obliged to take a civil oath. He is permitted to make a simple affirmation.

Now suppose I come to the door of Masonry and knock for admittance. Almost the first thing demanded of me is disobedience to the Lord Jesus. Before I can enter I must swear "to conceal and never reveal" any of the secrets of Masonry—things I yet know nothing about. It matters not that Christ has said, "Swear not at all." Masonry says, You *must swear*. For the true Christian there is but one response: "It is better to obey God than man."

Practically every Mason admits frankly that the taking of oaths is necessary to become a member, but I have met one or two who denied it. They said, "It is not an oath. It is only an obligation." One wonders what to think when one Mason says, "It is an oath," and another says, "It is not an oath." Somebody is wrong. We shall let this Masonic encyclopedia settle the matter. On page 522 Dr. Mackey discusses the "obligation of Masonic secrecy." He says the opponents of Masonry have brought five charges against this Masonic obligation of secrecy.

(1) It is an oath.

(2) It is administered before the secrets are communicated.

(3) It is accompanied by certain superstitious ceremonies.

(4) It is attended by a penalty.

26

(5) It is considered by the Masons as paramount to the obligations of the law of the land.

Mackey says further: "In replying to these statements, it is evident that the conscientious Freemason labors under great disadvantage. He is at every step restrained by his honor from either the denial or admission of his adversaries in relation to the mysteries of the Craft. But," he says, *"it may be granted, for the sake of argument, that every one of the first four charges is true"* (italics mine). The last charge, Mackey says, is "indignantly denied." But the first four are true!

Thus it is that Masonry with impunity asks men to disobey Jesus Christ, but at the same time it insists sternly that all its own mandates shall be obeyed immediately and implicitly. Page 525 points out:

> The first duty of every Mason is to obey the mandate of the master [not Christ, but the master of the Lodge]. This spirit of instant obedience and submission to authority constitutes the great safeguard of the Institution. . . . The order must be at once obeyed. Its character and its consequences may be matters of subsequent inquiry. The Masonic rule of obedience is like the nautical imperative: "Obey orders, even if you break owners."

Jesus Christ is the Owner of the Christian and the Christian must obey Him, not the profane voice of Masonry.

V. Masonry Teaches Its Members They May Reach Heaven, Life, and Immortality by a Way Apart from Jesus Christ.

If the Word of God teaches anything, it teaches that apart from Jesus Christ no man will ever reach heaven, see life, or receive immortality.

"Jesus saith unto him, I am the way, the truth, and the life: no man cometh unto the Father, but by me" (John 14:6).

"He that hath the Son hath life; and he that hath not the Son of God hath not life" (I John 5:12).

Masonry ignores Jesus Christ as the true Way of salvation. These Masonic books contain not the slightest hint which I can find that any Mason can be lost forever. But everywhere and always it is assumed that the Mason at death will enter the "temple not made with hands," receive eternal life, and enjoy immortality in the presence of God forever. It is assumed in the funeral ritual. It is assumed in the Masonic prayers. It is taught in Masonic symbolism. From the mass of testimony I choose one quotation. Among its other paraphernalia, Masonry has a ladder which is brought into the lodge for the work of initiation, so I was told by a Thirty-Second Degree Mason in good standing. On page 361 this encyclopedia gives the meaning of the ladder.

> This ladder is a symbol of progress . . .
> its three principal rounds, representing
> Faith, Hope, and Charity, present us
> with the means of advancing from earth
> to heaven, from death to life—from the
> mortal to immortality. Hence, its foot is
> placed on the ground floor of the Lodge,
> which is typical of the world, and its top
> rests on the covering of the Lodge, which
> is symbolic of heaven.

This is the Masonic way into heaven. The initiate is to climb into heaven by the ladder of Faith, Hope, and Charity. You say, "This sounds all right." But is it all right? Masonry has appropriated three beautiful words from the Bible, but what does Masonry mean by these words? Fortunately we are not left in the dark. The encyclopedia devotes an article to each word used in Masonry. "Faith" is faith in God (the god of Masonry). "Hope" is the hope of immortality. "Charity" is that love which the Mason shows toward brother Masons and fellow men.

Will such faith, hope, and charity save the soul of any man? You know it will not. If a man has nothing more than faith in God (and remember that the god of Masonry is not the true God), nothing more than hope for immortality, nothing is more certain than that that man will be lost. The devils believe in God and tremble! All men hope for immortality. Most men show some charity.

There is only one faith that can save—that is faith in the Lord Jesus Christ! There is only one hope that is sure—that is hope in the Lord Jesus Christ! There is only one charity which is recognized by God and rewarded—that is charity extended in the name of Jesus Christ!

The faith demanded by Masonry is not in Christ! The hope taught by Masonry is not in Christ! The charity inculcated by Masonry is not in the name of Christ. The ladder of Masonry is not the Way of Jesus Christ. The fact of the matter is that a man does not need a ladder to get into heaven! Praise the Lord. The entrance to heaven is not by a ladder. It is by a *Door!*

Jesus said: "I am the door: by me if any man enter in, he shall be saved." Now listen: "He that entereth not by the door . . . but climbeth up some other way [mark the words], the same is a thief and a robber" (John 10:1, 9). Any organization which ignores the Lord Jesus Christ as the Door of heaven, and puts up a ladder of its own, is a thief and a robber! Christ said that!

The way of Masonry is not the Way of the Cross. It is the way of human works and human character.

Speaking of the "working tools" of the "Entered Apprentice," Mackey says:

> THE COMMON GAVEL is an instrument made use of by operative masons to break off the corners of rough stones, the better to fit them for the builder's use; but we, as Free and Accepted Masons, are taught to make use of it for the more noble and glorious purpose of divesting our hearts and consciences of all the vices and superfluities of life; thereby fitting our minds as living stones for that spiritual building, that "house not made with hands" eternal in the heavens (The Ritualist, p. 39).

Oh, my friends, let me tell you upon the authority of God's Word that you can never get rid of your sins and vices with the "common gavel" of Masonry! You can never fit yourself for "the house not made with hands, eternal in the heavens." There is just one thing that can take away sins and make you fit to enter the blessed house—*the blood of Jesus Christ!* "Unto him that loved us, and washed us from our sins in his own blood . . . to him be glory and dominion for ever and ever. Amen" (Rev. 1:5-6).

You say, "If Masonry is such a terrible institution, why don't other men condemn it?" They do. John Adams condemned it! Also John Quincy Adams, James Madison, Millard Fillmore, Daniel Webster, Charles Sumner. Of the great evangelists, Finney condemned it. Moody condemned it. Torrey said: "I do not believe it is possible for a man to be an intelligent Christian and an intelligent Mason at the same time." George F. Pentecost, late pastor of the Wanamaker Church in this city, said, "I believe that Masonry is an incalculable evil and essentially antichrist in its principles and influences." He should have known something about it, for a Thirty-Second Degree Mason told me last week that church had a lodge within its own membership.

Why do Christian men stay in it? I can think of only four reasons why you find professing Christians affiliated with the Masonic lodge:

First—Some do not know what Christianity really is. Many have the prevalent but erroneous opinion that Christianity and religion are one and the same thing. If an organization is religious and talks about

God, they conclude it is Christian. Such people are sincere but untaught. Because they do not know what Christianity is, they see nothing wrong with Masonry. These deserve our sympathy. If there is to be any blame, it belongs to the pastors who have failed to teach them the truth.

Second—Some do not know what Masonry really is. It is possible that some here may scoff at the idea of a Mason not knowing what his lodge stands for. Nevertheless, it is true that there are thousands of Masons who are not acquainted with the religious position of Masonry as an institution. I have met Thirty-Second Degree Masons who frankly admitted that they had never read even one Masonic authority such as this encyclopedia. Within the past month I have actually found Masons who denied the existence of such works! Yet the Masonic Temple of this city has a fair-sized library of books on Masonry, many of which are accessible to the non-Masonic public.

You may think that such ignorance is impossible. Not at all! You find it in every organization. I think I could find members of the Brethren church here at this place who have never read a book setting forth the position of the denomination and who would be unable to state it. It is the same in every church, whether Presbyterian, Methodist, or Baptist. If such ignorance can be found in organizations where public instruction is given several times each week, it is not surprising to find it in Masonry. The average Mason is like some church members. He only does what is absolutely necessary to become a member and stops there. His knowledge of Masonry is based upon his little experience in a local lodge, and he never makes any effort to ascertain exactly what is the religious position of Masonry as a great institution.

Permit me to say in all kindness, that the gentleman who rose at the beginning of this sermon to protest against the charge that Masonry is not Christian is an illustration of what I am saying. He has admitted before you all, in answer to my question, that *he has never read even one Masonic authority.* We have no denunciation for such men, but in the name of Jesus Christ we beg that they will investigate the institution to which they are giving their allegiance.

Third—A few professing Christians continue their relation with Masonry in spite of the fact that they know what Christianity is, and also what Masonry is. Such as these are without excuse. They are living every day in deliberate disloyalty to the Lord Jesus Christ, who died for their sins! They deserve blame, not sympathy.

Fourth—There are some professing Christians in

Masonry who are apostate from the true faith.
Some of the preachers in Masonry belong in this classification. They have relegated such truths as blood atonement and the deity of Christ to the place of nonessentials. They are virtually Unitarian in belief, and, therefore, it is not surprising to find them in an institution which in its three main degrees is Unitarianism, so much so that ex-President Taft, a prominent Unitarian, feels at home in it. The presence of such men in Masonry is an argument against it, not for it.

"But," you say, "there are good men in it. Washington was a Mason." Yes; and Washington was a slave-owner also. You are not to follow men. If you follow men you are heading for disaster. Christ says to the Christian, "Follow thou me."

I must close, though I have only begun. This encyclopedia contains enough that is anti-Christian to keep me preaching for the next ten weeks every Sunday night. I have said enough to condemn this institution forever in the eyes of you who know Jesus Christ and love Him. I have tried not to be harsh or unkind. I have tried to tell you the truth. Jesus Christ is the only hope for men. My only motive tonight has been to get you to be loyal to Him. A man may say: "It will hurt me if I leave Masonry now!" I know it will! But oh, Christian, did your Christ fail you at the cross because it hurt?

By the blood of His cross I plead with you: "Come out from among them, and be ye separate." "Be ye not unequally yoked together with unbelievers: for what fellowship hath righteousness with unrighteousness? and what communion hath light with darkness? And what concord hath Christ with Belial? or what part hath he that believeth with an infidel? And what agreement hath the temple of God with idols? . . ." (II Cor. 6:14-17).